KU-527-082

Climbing
Roses

Among all floures of the worlde the floure

of the rose is chief and beeryth ye pryse.

And by cause of vertues and swete smelle

and savour. For by fayrnesse they fede the

syghte; and playseth the smelle by odour,

the touche by softe handlynge.

And wythstondeth and socouryth by

vertue agenst many syknesses and evylles.

BARTHOLOMAEUS ANGLICUS:
De Proprietatibus Rerum, 1495

β

ACKNOWLEDGEMENTS

Many people helped to make this book, too many to mention everyone
individually, but special thanks must go to Sue Gernæy for her comments,
advice and contributions, Ian Thraves for taking many of the rose portraits
and David Austin Roses and Keith Jones of C & K Jones for all their help with
photography. Also thanks to Chris & Barbara Warner for the illuminating tour
of Warner's Roses and the hybridisation process, Valerie Lewis Chandler for
proofing and indexing, and John Miles for guidance on design. Finally,
the many photographers and photo libraries whose work we have kindly
received permission to reproduce are credited individually on page 63.

First published in Great Britain in 2000
Second impression 2000
Parsimony Press Limited
West Huntspill, Somerset

A CIP catalogue record for this book is available from the British Library

ISBN 1 902979 00 1

Editor: Caroline Russell
Typesetting & design: Olivia Norton
Colour reproduction: Colourpath, London
Printed and bound by: Poligrafico Dehoniano, Italy

The buttons

NO GARDEN?

CONTAINER

*Can be grown in container given right conditions
(see page 8)*

FLOWERING PERIOD

CONTINUOUS

*Flowers all season
(usually summer to late autumn)*

REPEAT FLOWERING

*Flowers at the beginning of the summer and then
again late summer/early autumn*

SUMMER FLOWERING

*Flowers once (although sometimes prolonged display)
usually in June/July*

SPRING FLOWERING

Flowers in late Spring

FRAGRANCE

VERY FRAGRANT

Incredible perfume

FRAGRANT

Very pleasant and noticeable scent

SLIGHTLY FRAGRANT

*Probably have to give the flower a good sniff
to get any joy*

ASPECT

NORTH-FACING

Will tolerate a north-facing position

SOIL

POOR SOIL

Will tolerate poorer soils

DISEASE

DISEASE RESISTANT

*Has good disease resistance
(but still needs tender loving care)*

DIMMED BUTTONS

The characteristic at issue is not applicable

Contents

IT BECAME APPARENT while researching this little book, that among rose devotees there are almost as many opinions as there are varieties. A rose some people consider has an extraordinary fragrance to others has no discernable smell. Estimates on eventual height vary widely, and in the matter of aesthetics, not surprisingly, one man's meat is invariably another man's poison. Rather than trying to unravel these disparities, consider that one of the most wonderful things about roses is they come in so many shapes and sizes, colours and perfumes that we can all find one that appeals. It is you who have to live with the rose and who know where you might like to plant it. This guide is supposed to be a starting point, not a 'bible'. It is by no means a comprehensive list, but does include some of the nation's favourites, some of ours and, for those who already know a good deal, some newcomers. Stick it in your pocket to read on a train, or take with you when visiting a garden or nursery. It will also fit in an envelope to be sent to that difficult-to-buy-for uncle, as a present.

'New Dawn' cascading over arch at Charleston Manor

The descriptions are unashamedly cursory. We concentrate on photographs and which questions are most often asked when trying to choose a climbing rose, and then arrange the answers in 'buttons' down the side of the page for easy reference. However, and this may seem an odd thing to write when trying flog a book, nothing beats going out and seeing (and smelling) the real thing, established and happy, growing through a tree or covering a house, being inspired not only by the roses but the people who grow them and who are often all too happy to pass on their knowledge to the uninitiated.

At the back of the book is a shortlist of gardens and nurseries that may be of interest and a bibliography of some of the best books on roses and plant reference guides, and to whose authors and editors we are indebted. Many of you will be familiar with these titles already. If not, you are in for a treat. Two short sections on companion plants and a cross-reference of roses for particular situations are also included.

'Compassion' growing through tree

The differences between climbers and ramblers

A somewhat arbitrary division, but useful to know particularly for pruning purposes.

RAMBLERS generally flower only once in the season (summer flowering), usually some time during June or July. The new stems, which come from the base of the plant and will carry the following season's flowers, are pliable and lax, often carrying clusters of smaller flowers, and are particularly suitable for training over fences, pergolas, growing into trees and for disguising ugly buildings.

CLIMBERS usually have the capacity to flower more than once during the season (repeat flowering), and some flower continuously. The flowers which are produced on the current season's stems are usually larger than ramblers'. The stems are more rigid and will need training to make a permanent framework.

Both have their strengths. Luckily, neither nature nor rose breeders will have it so black and white, so there are, of course, exceptions. These are noted in the individual entries.

Choosing climbing roses

This can be a daunting task, especially if your garden is not a large one and only has room for one or two. Where this is the case it is important that every plant should 'sing for its supper', so a rose which is not only scented but flowers continuously *and* is your favourite colour is an obvious first choice.

Surprisingly, only a tiny selection of climbing roses are available in general garden centres. For this reason a number of rose specialist nurseries are listed in this book. From them you can buy container-grown varieties in person or bare-root roses by mail.

Planting and maintenance

As boring as it is, if you just dig a hole, bung it in and hope for the best, you will rarely grow a happy rose. Treated this unkindly it is unlikely to thrive and will also be prone to disease. Ideally, roses like a sunny, sheltered spot, a rich, slightly acidic loamy soil and good drainage, but most will accept less than perfect conditions given some help. Before you even think of planting, the soil should be well prepared (I hear a groan). Dig the ground deeply, getting rid of the weeds, and mix some well rotted manure or compost and a handful of bonemeal in with the soil. Be generous with the amount of humus you mix in with chalky (alkaline) soil, which disagrees with roses, and causes the leaves to yellow (chlorosis). It makes sense that when planting in existing rosebeds, or replacing a rose, particularly if it died of something nasty, you should replace the soil to a depth of at least 18in (50cm) and a width of 2ft (60cm). Its predecessor will have used up most of the nutrients, and the chances of passing on diseases will be reduced. If this is too much trouble, choose another spot and 'rest' the ground for three or four years.

The best time to plant roses is when they are dormant (i.e. from November to the end of March). This is when your bare-rooted, mail order roses will arrive. Set the rose in the hole about 18 ins (45cm) away from the wall or support, at an angle of 45° and spread out the roots evenly. Check that the bud union (the point where the shoots join the root stock) is about an inch (2.5cm) below the final soil level. Replace the soil, without leaving air pockets, and firm down gently. Water well.

If it's very wet or frosty, the roses can be 'heeled in', by putting them in a shallow trench with the earth lightly compacted around them, until conditions have improved. If you have no spare ground to do this, keep the roots moist and store in a cool but frost-free place.

If you miss the 'bare-root' boat, or like many of us do not think about your garden until the weather improves, container-grown roses can be bought from spring until early autumn. The procedure for site preparation is the same (that little bit of earth around the roots does not excuse you). When planting a container-grown rose, water well beforehand and do not disturb the root ball.

When planting against a tree, the rose should be planted on the side of the prevailing wind and should be supported until it reaches the branches into which it will eventually become entwined. Trees that are past their best are ideal, though they must be strong enough to support the weight of the more vigorous varieties.

Ramblers are prone to mildew, so are best planted in positions that allow good air circulation i.e. not the walls of a house. A pergola, tree, fence or trellis would be a better choice and also show off their hanging clusters of flowers to good effect. Climbing roses, having a stiffer habit, are best on walls or fences, but if trained properly in the early years can be grown on most structures.

As far as **maintenance** goes – your rose will love you if you rake up the fallen leaves, and mulch with leaf mould or garden compost in the autumn to prevent the spread of diseases. Add well-rotted manure or leaf mould in the spring to improve the structure of the soil and help retain moisture. Water well, especially in the first few years, particularly in dry spells, but do not overwater as the roots don't like to be waterlogged. A plant in vigorous health is much less likely to become diseased and so saves messing about with unpleasant sprays or having to read the *Pests and Diseases* section (p. 9).

Growing climbing roses in containers

This is possible, but smaller climbing roses (under 10ft/3m) are probably the best bet. The size of the pot is also an important consideration, dictating the final height of the rose. Be as generous as you can, but nothing less than 25 litre capacity or 2 ft (60cm) depth should be used. Ample drainage, not allowing the soil to dry out, and regular feeding are also essential.

Training, pruning and deadheading

Deadhead when the flowers become unsightly, unless the hips are decorative. Snip the stalk at the second or third leaf below the flower.

Pruning is not the complicated business it is sometimes made out to be, much of it coming down to common sense; but the timing and process are slightly different for climbing and rambling roses.

Because **climbers** produce flowers on the new growth, for the first two years you should be making a framework by training the new shoots, ideally along horizontal supports, only gently thinning out anything dead, diseased or straggly-looking. From about the third year, in late winter to spring, you are trying to keep the main stems within the area you have allotted and pruning back the side-shoots by about two thirds of their length, leaving two or three buds. If the main framework begins to look a bit bare, cut one or two of the oldest shoots back to 12 ins (30cm) from the ground.

Some are of the opinion that you can just leave **ramblers** to their own devices, but this does depend on vigour and available space. If you need to prune tangled or overreaching roses, do so in late summer after flowering, because ramblers produce flowers from the previous season's growth. For the first two years concentrate on training the new shoots onto horizontal wires or other support, and only prune the side shoots back to 2-4 buds. From the third year, you can cut out about a quarter to a third of the stems that have flowered back down to the base (you will probably have to do this in sections) tying in the new growth, from which next year's flowers will be produced, to your support. Training horizontally encourages flowering all along the main stems.

In both cases **suckers** should also be removed as they can take over the whole plant. They are shoots that grow from the rootstock (i.e. below the union) rather than the rose that has been grafted on to it – easy to spot, usually being stronger growers with different leaves.

Pests and diseases

An often under-rated pest is the domestic animal. Dogs, whose brains decrease in proportion to the length and floppiness of their ears, can cause havoc, especially when they are young and bouncy. Young and bouncy children can also do their share of damage, but their depredations are to some extent limited by the fact that nature gave roses thorns for protection. As for the smaller pests and diseases, you can throw money and chemistry at the problem, but in the long run it is cheaper (and more organic) just to rake up the fallen leaves in autumn and mulch with leaf mould or garden compost to prevent diseases spreading. Brief mention to companion planting as a combatant is explained on page 58. If you do resort to sprays, use one of the proprietary fungicides on the market for the specific disease and an insecticide for the pests. For all the fungal diseases, at the first sign, before you get an infestation, it is worth removing the infected leaves by hand and burning them. The problems you are most likely to encounter are:

BLACK SPOT

A fungal disease, more common in South-West England and South Wales.
Brownish–black spots appear on the leaves in June and spread rapidly, causing the leaves to turn yellow and drop off. Poor drainage and too much shade are often the cause. You can spray with a fungicide at intervals starting in spring. Garlic and chives have some fungicidal properties as well as deterring greenfly, so make excellent companions for roses.

ROSE RUST

A serious fungal disease more common in the South and South East.
Orange coloured spores appear on the undersides of the leaves. In late summer the spores turn black causing the leaves to fall prematurely and therefore weakening the plant. It is much more common in overcrowded and neglected plants. Prevention is much better than cure here, the spores overwinter on fallen leaves, so it is essential that they are raked up and burned. If you need to spray, use a fungicide on the underside of the leaves.

ROSE OR POWDERY MILDEW

Very common.

White powdery mould appears on young leaves and buds during summer or early autumn. If plant becomes very heavily infected, the leaves will turn yellow and drop off and the buds will fail to open. Mildew thrives in dry, airless conditions, so make sure plants are fed, watered and not overcrowded. If it is a regular problem, you could spray with a fungicide as soon as the disease appears.

APHIDS (GREENFLY)

Easy to spot, as they cluster together feeding on the young tips of growing shoots, usually in great numbers. Blue tits, ladybirds and hoverflies are very partial to aphids so if you use an insecticide, choose one that is not harmful to them, or an insecticidal soap spray. Alternatively, chives or garlic act as a useful and pungent deterrent. Underplanting with something like cranesbill geraniums or, it has to be admitted the much less elegant *Limnanthes douglasii* (poached egg plant) will be appreciated by your most efficient ally against the aphid, the hoverfly.

LEAF-ROLLING SAWFLY

The leaves curl up and a pale green grub can be found inside. Too much shade can be the cause, and it is unsightly but there are far worse problems to have in life. One can remove the grubs by hand, but once the leaves have curled, there is not much one can do about it. Some advocate preventative spraying the following year, but surely a much nicer long-term solution is a couple of blue tit nesting boxes?

VERY OFTEN, the site in which you wish to plant your rose is the deciding factor in which rose to buy. Nurseries are always being asked to advise on this. Using the most commonly-asked questions as a starting point, all the roses in this book have been graded by the characteristics which seem to matter most to us. These icons and buttons have been arranged down the side of each rose entry to act as a quick reference when making a short-list of possible contenders for a place in your garden.

The icons

POSITION

Needs a sunny position

Will tolerate only half a day's sun, but give it the most you can

CLIMATE

Half-hardy
Can withstand temperatures down to 0°C (32°F)

Frost hardy
Can withstand temperatures down to -5°C (23°F)

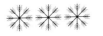

Fully hardy
Can withstand temperatures down to -15°C (5°F)

SIZE

00ft (00m)

Height of plant from ground

◀ 00ft (00m) ▶

Spread of plant

The buttons

NO GARDEN?

CONTAINER *Can be grown in container given right conditions (see page 8)*

FLOWERING PERIOD

CONTINUOUS *Flowers all season (usually summer to late autumn)*

REPEAT FLOWERING *Flowers at the beginning of the summer and then again late summer/early autumn*

_____ *Flowers once (although sometimes prolonged display) usually in June/July*

_____ *Flowers in late Spring*

FRAGRANCE

VERY FRAGRANT *Incredible perfume*

FRAGRANT *Very pleasant and noticeable scent*

SLIGHTLY FRAGRANT *Probably have to give the flower a good sniff to get any joy*

ASPECT

NORTH-FACING *Will tolerate a north-facing position*

SOIL

POOR SOIL *Will tolerate poorer soils*

DISEASE

DISEASE RESISTANT *Has good disease resistance (but still needs tender loving care)*

DIMMED BUTTONS

The characteristic at issue is not applicable

13

SKILL AND THE THROW of the dice both play a part in the advent of new varieties. Breeders will have an idea of the characteristics they wish to retain and combine, but there is no guarantee they will succeed. It is similar to having a baby: it may be hoped the child will have his blue eyes and her small nose, but the big-nosed, brown-eyed reality frequently has its own unpredictable charm.

Every so often a plant may deviate from its normal type, without any human intervention, and produce what is called a 'sport'. The differences from its parent may be striking or subtle but many lovely roses have appeared in this fashion. Furthermore, this means new varieties are not confined to the territory of the professionals. A lucky (and observant) amateur gardener may discover such an addition among his or her roses. However, all the roses in this section are the progeny of expert rose growers. Practical considerations, such as disease resistance, suitability for small gardens and the ability to flower continuously right through the summer have played a part in their make-up, but not to the detriment of their looks. Some have the more formal, sculptured shapes and brighter colours often associated with 'modern roses', but there is also a great deal to be said for those retaining something of the grace, simple beauty and subtle shades of their forebears.

This selection is particularly suited to the modern, small garden or smaller spaces within a larger one – some are even suitable for a container of sufficiently generous proportions. Although they haven't been around long enough to develop a reputation, given the basic care outlined on pages 7-11, they are easy to grow, and should thrive for many years.

'Little Rambler'

PENNY LANE
('Hardwell')

13ft (4m)

◀ 7ft (2.2m) ▶

CLASSIFICATION: Climber (Modern)

ORIGIN: Harkness (1998)

COLOUR: Honey-champagne paling to pearl

BLOOM SIZE: Large – 3-4in (8-10cm)

FOLIAGE: Dense, dark, polished green

GOOD FOR: Wall, fence, pergola, pillar, flowers good for cutting

This is the first climber to be chosen as Rose of the Year, an award delivered jointly by the British Associations of Growers and Breeders. An accolade that tells us this rose is not only beautiful, but also healthy, reliable and easy to grow. Its lovely fragrance much improved an hour and a half car journey on the way back from the nursery. The growth is quite lax, so it is easily trained and the dark, polished leaves set off the pale blooms very well. The blooms are at their most perfect in the early stages, but even the elderly flowers never seem to look horrid, just a bit more ruffled, and informal.

SNOW GOOSE
('Auspom')

▲
8ft (2.5m)
▼

◀ 10ft (3m) ▶

CLASSIFICATION: Rambler
ORIGIN: David Austin (1996)
COLOUR: White with yellow stamens
BLOOM SIZE: Small – 1½in (4cm)
FOLIAGE: Semi-glossy, mid-green pointed leaflets
GOOD FOR: Arch, pergola, pillar, wall or fence
  in small gardens

CONTAINER

CONTINUOUS

FRAGRANT

DISEASE RESISTANT

Dense clusters of small, delicate, tissue-paper
blooms make it difficult to resist this rose. In fact,
its fragile appearance belies a tough, disease-resistant
physique, escaping the problems with mildew to
which so many ramblers are prone. Its manageable
size makes it a good choice for a small garden, and
it is very pretty grown over an arch, where the
splendid combination of a rambler-like habit with
summer-long, scented flowers will be shown off to
best advantage. It prefers a sunny position but will
be all right given half a day of sunshine.

LITTLE RAMBLER
('Chewramb')

7ft (2.2m)

◀ 7ft (2.2m) ▶

CONTAINER

CONTINUOUS

FRAGRANT

DISEASE RESISTANT

CLASSIFICATION: Rambler
ORIGIN: Warner (1994)
COLOUR: Blush pink, almost white,
   yellow stamens
BLOOM SIZE: Small – 2in (5cm)
FOLIAGE: Small, semi-glossy dark green
GOOD FOR: Low fence, wall, trellis or pillar in
   small gardens, restricted spaces

Its moderate growth is the reason why this is
sometimes called a 'patio climber' in the rose
catalogues. A better reason to grow it on a patio,
close to the house, or somewhere you can sit out and
enjoy it is its heavenly fragrance. On a more
practical level, it is an excellent choice to fill a small
space as its sideways habit means it can spread as
wide as it grows tall. All along its pliable stems,
generous clusters of small flowers are produced all
summer long, normally unheard of in a rambler. As
it matures it becomes even more prolific, so the
overall effect is stunning. The dark foliage looks
semi-glossy and healthy, as indeed it is, having
excellent disease resistance.

NICE DAY
('Chewsea')

7ft (2.2m)

◀ 3ft (1m) ▶

CLASSIFICATION: Climber (Modern)
ORIGIN: Warner (1994)
COLOUR: Salmon-tinted pink
BLOOM SIZE: Small – 2in (5cm)
FOLIAGE: Glossy, dark green
GOOD FOR: Small gardens, low wall,
for cut flowers

CONTAINER

CONTINUOUS

FRAGRANT

An unusual looking miniature climber, with
pointed petals arranged in neat, orderly layers, to
form a fully double flower. The central part of each
petal is salmon, the edge pink. This juxtaposition
gives the flower a luminous quality which is very
striking. There is a distinctive, sweet fragrance, but
not enough to carry far. Good for brightening a
small space and particularly fine against a dark
background. This can be grown in a large (at least
25 litre) container. Despite not having the same
high level of disease resistance as others of Chris
Warner's roses, this has proved to be a popular and
striking newcomer.

WARM WELCOME
('Chewizz')

7ft (2.2m)

◀ 7ft (2.2m) ▶

CONTAINER

CONTINUOUS

SLIGHTLY FRAGRANT

DISEASE RESISTANT

CLASSIFICATION: Climber (Modern)
ORIGIN: Warner (1991)
COLOUR: Orange-vermilion, yellow at the centre
BLOOM SIZE: Small – 2in (5cm)
FOLIAGE: Plentiful, dark green
GOOD FOR: Wall, fence, pillar or small arch

Nothing shy and retiring about this one either. It is particularly good for confined spaces, as its growth is quite short and upright, though not too stiff. The blooms are continuous, into winter, and are borne in clusters. It does not score as highly on fragrance as some of the other roses, but what it lacks in fragrance it makes up for in colour. This may be bright, but is balanced by the small simple flower shape and dark foliage and so doesn't look garish or overdone, just cheerful. This is a fabulous rose.

GOOD AS GOLD
('Chewsunbeam')

7ft (2.2m)

5ft (1.5m)

CLASSIFICATION: Climber (Modern)
ORIGIN: Warner (1995)
COLOUR: Golden yellow
BLOOM SIZE: Medium – 2-3in (5-8cm)
FOLIAGE: Dark green, glossy, small
GOOD FOR: Wall, fence or pillar, smaller gardens

CONTAINER

CONTINUOUS

FRAGRANT

DISEASE RESISTANT

It begins to look like a fix. Another rose from Chris Warner. However, his high standards mean that the punter gets roses that have good disease resistance and a generous coverage of blooms from top to bottom of the plant – both characteristics not to be sniffed at. Its clear yellow blooms, with a sweet but not overpowering fragrance, appear in generous clusters throughout summer. It only reaches around 7ft but again this makes it a good choice for the smaller garden.

AMBIVALENCE IS NOT the standard response to the roses in this section! There is no denying the attractiveness and subtlety of some of the pale pink, white and yellow roses which make such comfortable companions to the traditional plants of the English country garden — but for those who want to experiment a little with bolder colour schemes, or who are just looking for a splash of bright summer colour, here is a small selection of the 'hottest' reds, carmines, yellows and oranges, some with the added advantage of fragrance.

Those that flower only once can make way for other plants and a changing colour scheme, but for those that flower continuously, we have chosen varieties, particularly of the reds, that are unfading. Additionally, we have already described two roses in the section *Nineties Newcomers* that would fit well here – 'Warm Welcome', a brilliant orange-vermilion and 'Good as Gold', clear yellow. The *Tough as Old Boots* section offers two further rather delicious reds in 'Crimson Shower' and 'Étoile de Hollande, Climbing'.

Although a riot of colour is an appealing proposition, it takes skill to achieve. Novices might want to steer clear of mixing many shades of the same colour, unless they are happy to learn by trial and error (or *want* to drive out their neighbours). Get ideas by walking around 'real-life' gardens. A day at Mottisfont will be remembered long after a bank holiday dash into a garden centre. Less costly and just as enjoyable can be the opening of a small local garden under the National Gardens Scheme (p. 59)

The picture opposite shows a thriving 'Dublin Bay'. Its projected height is about 7ft, but unconstrained, it is racing towards the roof – with energy left for blooms!

'Dublin Bay' trained on cottage wall, July

ALTISSIMO

12ft (3.7m)

◀ 8ft (2.5m) ▶

CONTINUOUS

SLIGHTLY FRAGRANT

CLASSIFICATION: Climber
ORIGIN: Delbard-Chabert (1966)
COLOUR: Blood red, shaded with crimson,
  golden stamens
BLOOM SIZE: Large – 5in (12cm)
FOLIAGE: Large-leaved, matt, dark green
GOOD FOR: Open site, pillar, trellis,
  fence or arch

There is something very attractive about the
simplicity of single flowers. Combine this with
the deep unfading red of the blooms and an ability
to repeat flower well, this rose is certainly worthy
of consideration if summer-long colour is required.
It will clash with a red-brick wall, but looks well
against a foil of green, healthy foliage. Because of
its upright habit, this one would look particularly
good growing up a pillar. There is only a slight
fragrance, however; were it not for this it would
probably be more popular.

ALEXANDER GIRAULT

15ft (4.6m)

◀ 12ft (3.7m) ▶

CLASSIFICATION: Rambler
ORIGIN: Barbier, France (1909)
COLOUR: Reddish-pink
BLOOM SIZE: Small – 2in (5cm)
FOLIAGE: Dark and glossy
GOOD FOR: Growing through trees,
    a very large trellis

VERY FRAGRANT

POOR SOIL

The buds are tinted red, but the flowers open to a
very strong shade of carmine with yellow stamens
and a green eye. In the mass, the effect is stunning.
With a vigorous habit, it should not be confined in a
small space, it can reach 20ft in perfect conditions
but 12-15 is more usual. Being a rambler, the wall
of a house might not provide enough circulation to
prevent mildew but choosing a position near to the
house to take advantage of its delicious scent would
be a good move. Not too prickly.

DUBLIN BAY

7ft (2.2m)

◀ 6ft (1.8m) ▶

CONTAINER

CONTINUOUS

SLIGHTLY FRAGRANT

POOR SOIL

DISEASE RESISTANT

CLASSIFICATION: Climber (Modern)
ORIGIN: McGredy (1976)
COLOUR: Bright, rich red
BLOOM SIZE: Large – 4in (10cm)
FOLIAGE: Glossy, darkish-green
GOOD FOR: Pillar, wall or hedging,
    smaller gardens

The colour is the thing. Many people have a large
soft spot for the truly red rose, and this is a good
example of glorious and unfading variety. Its smaller
stature and continuous flowering, make it a good
choice for the smaller garden or a front garden
where it will cheer up the street long after other
varieties have given up. Add to this a pleasant but
not strong fragrance, disease resistance and ability to
thrive in a variety of conditions and you can forgive
its lack of elegance. Its lively disposition is well
illustrated in the photograph on page 23.

ORANGE SUNBLAZE, CLIMBING
('Meijikatarsar')

5ft (1.5m)

◀ **4ft (1.2m)** ▶

CLASSIFICATION: Climber (Modern)
ORIGIN: Meilland (1986)
COLOUR: Bright orange-red
BLOOM SIZE: Small – 1½ in (4cm)
FOLIAGE: Pointed, glossy, dark green
GOOD FOR: Confined spaces, container

CONTAINER

CONTINUOUS

SLIGHTLY FRAGRANT

This is a climbing sport of the miniature rose
Orange Sunblaze. It may not grow to a great height
or spread very wide, but it makes its presence felt by
blooming profusely all through summer all over the
plant. This makes it an ideal choice where space is
limited. All this flowering, however, takes energy, so
if you want it to excel, give it fertile soil and an
open site. Of all the roses in this section, this one
will probably get the strongest reaction. For some its
vibrant colouring and diminutive stature is different
and therefore exciting, for others it inspires nothing
short of revulsion.

GOLDEN SHOWERS

8ft (2.5m)

◀ 7ft (2.2m) ▶

CONTAINER

CONTINUOUS

FRAGRANT

NORTH-FACING

POOR SOIL

DISEASE RESISTANT

CLASSIFICATION: Climber (Modern)
ORIGIN: Lammerts (1956)
COLOUR: Bright yellow
BLOOM SIZE: Large – 4in (10cm)
FOLIAGE: Dark, glossy green
GOOD FOR: Wall, pillar or arch

The loose ruffled petals will fade later to a creamy yellow, especially in hot sun, but this doesn't create the sort of clashing problem that happens when a red bloom fades to a purple. Swathed in ruffled blooms from summer into autumn with a continuity that is matched by few other climbers, this is a very appealing rose. It has a lovely lemony fragrance to boot. It's excellent for a small garden and is a good choice for a north wall. Popular? Yes, very – you probably won't have to look far to buy this one. It is even for sale in some supermarkets.

MAIGOLD

10ft (3m)

8ft (2.5m)

CLASSIFICATION: Climber
ORIGIN: Kordes (1953)
COLOUR: Rich bronze yellow, golden stamens
BLOOM SIZE: Large – 4in (10cm)
FOLIAGE: Plentiful, rich, glossy-green
GOOD FOR: Wall, pergola, pillar,
    can be grown as shrub

CONTAINER

REPEAT FLOWERING

FRAGRANT

NORTH-FACING

POOR SOIL

DISEASE RESISTANT

At their best, the flowers are a powerful, no-nonsense yellow (although the buds are streaked with red) but it would be dishonest to pretend that the flowers always age well. Among its devotees are gardeners who want a rose for difficult conditions, as it will tolerate a range of soils and even an exposed site or light shade. It is hardy and disease resistant and its first crop of blooms, usually in May, will be generous and perhaps last for six weeks. The later blooms come less freely and will not come at all if not dead-headed. It has a musky scent and sharp prickles!

ORIGINALLY, WHEN PUTTING together this book, our policy was to include roses that were problem-free and fully hardy so that even someone with no experience of gardening might feel inspired to grow one of them. However, it soon became apparent that this deprived us of roses that were too beautiful or unique to leave out.

Ostensibly, all the roses in this section are tender and may not survive a bad winter and some need the warmth of the sun to flourish. Having said that, given love and affection and proper consideration when deciding where to plant you can shorten the odds, outwit the elements and enjoy the very particular pleasure of rising to a challenge. None of these is so handicapped that you are backing a loser, and look at what there is to gain.

When choosing *where* to plant, it is worth bearing in mind that after a frost, a plant may survive a slow thaw as the temperature rises gradually, but if sunlight falls on the plant too early in the day, the thaw will be too quick and is much more likely to do serious damage. Thus an east-facing wall, even though it's warmer than a north-facing one, could be the very worst position to choose. For most of these, a sheltered south-facing wall of a house would probably be the best bet.

The *Rosa banksiae* 'Lutea', right, chosen to illustrate this section, gives some idea of how breathtakingly lovely a rambler can be, and why so many people cite Banksian roses as favourites. Seduced by this mass of tiny, nodding, clusters of flowers, you just don't care that it's usually all over by the middle of June. But try and avoid temptation if you have a small garden, as it needs to have its head. Best to make a pilgrimage to someone else's every spring, and fall for one of the other varieties in this section instead.

Rosa banksiae *'Lutea'*

R. BANKSIAE 'LUTEA'
('Yellow Banksian')

30ft (9.2m)

25ft (7.6m)

SLIGHTLY FRAGRANT

CLASSIFICATION: Rambler

ORIGIN: Brought from China by JD Park
(RHS 1824)

COLOUR: Deep yellow

BLOOM SIZE: Small – ¾ inch (1cm)

FOLIAGE: Abundant, matt, light green

GOOD FOR: South or west wall of a house, or
tree in a favoured area

The 'Banksian roses' form a group of some of
the loveliest of climbers. They are native to China
and were discovered and brought to England in
the nineteenth century. There is no doubt that *Rosa
banksiae* 'Lutea' is quite glorious, in full bloom in
late May and early June, particularly when mature
enough to have reached the roof of the house. Very
special and worth the effort, it is a little tender and
needs a sheltered, warm spot. Blooms are formed on
the second and third year's growth so keep pruning
to the minimum. It is reputedly the hardiest of the
Banksian roses in our climate, and is therefore easier
to find.

ALISTER STELLA GRAY
('Golden Rambler')

15ft (4.6m)

◀ 10ft (3m) ▶

CLASSIFICATION: Climber

ORIGIN: Gray (1894)

COLOUR: Yolk-yellow buds fading to creamy white flowers

BLOOM SIZE: Medium – 2½in (6cm)

FOLIAGE: Thick, smooth, dark green

GOOD FOR: Wall, arch, pergola, trellis, cutting and buttonholes

REPEAT FLOWERING

VERY FRAGRANT

A very bad winter might deprive you of this rose, but otherwise, planted in a sheltered site it's a good bet it will be safe. The warmth of the sun also gives the flowers a better colour. Charming, scrolled buds, delicate flowers with silky petals, a fabulous tea-rose fragrance and the ability to repeat-flower tick a lot of boxes on the 'plus' side. When it is in full flower, the effect of the range of shades is quite stunning, and quite often its second flush is superior to the earlier one. Graham Stuart Thomas writes most warmly of this rose, remembering, as a child, his father picking a buttonhole almost every day from July to October. If, after this list of accolades you need further persuasion – it is practically thornless.

MERMAID

20ft (6.1m)

◀ 20ft (6.1m) ▶

CLASSIFICATION: Climber

ORIGIN: Paul (1918)

COLOUR: Canary-yellow, sulphur stamens

BLOOM SIZE: Large – 5in (13cm)

FOLIAGE: Semi-evergreen, glossy, dark green

GOOD FOR: Very big wall, preferably
south or west aspect

A bit of an interloper. Officially 'Mermaid' is
tender. However, surprisingly, it often does well on
a north-facing wall and is semi-evergreen in a mild
winter. It is not a rose for instant gratification. It
takes a while to get going and resents pruning after
it has. But it will reward you with these lovely
waved petals, a thick boss of golden stamens which
remain after the petals have fallen and a sweet
delicate scent. Its hooked thorns are razor sharp, so
it's perfect for keeping out intruders! Luckily, it is
advised to keep pruning to a minimum, so you
won't have to tackle it too often, but there are some
notably Christopher Lloyd, who think this is reason
enough to eschew it.

LADY HILLINGDON, CLIMBING

15ft (4.6m)

◀ 8ft (2.5m) ▶

CONTINUOUS

VERY FRAGRANT

CLASSIFICATION: Climber
ORIGIN: Hicks (1917)
COLOUR: Light apricot-yellow
BLOOM SIZE: Med – 3½in (9cm)
FOLIAGE: Glossy, dark green
GOOD FOR: Warm wall, sheltered site,
    flowers good for cutting

When we say apricot-yellow, we mean it.
This is probably the truest match to the lovely
golden tones of the fruit that you can find amongst
the climbers. It is a sport of the tea rose 'Lady
Hillingdon', and this is where it gets its tenderness,
but also its marvellous fragrance, rich and fruity, and
the slender, elegant, shapely buds. The flowers are
borne in sprays and repeat regularly through the
summer. The new leaves are tinted reddish-purple
becoming large, dark and glossy as they mature.
There is some dispute about whether it is repeat
flowering or continuous, but in practice it seems
pretty continuous.

RAMONA
('Red Cherokee')

10ft (3m)

◀ 8ft (2.5m) ▶

SLIGHTLY FRAGRANT

CLASSIFICATION: Rambler

ORIGIN: Discovered by Dietrich and Turner (1913)

COLOUR: Cerise-crimson with golden stamens

BLOOM SIZE: Large – 4in (10cm)

FOLIAGE: Sparse, dark green, glossy

GOOD FOR: Warm, sheltered wall

It is difficult to match the simple, delicate beauty of species (or wild) roses. This hybrid is a sport from *Rosa anemonoides* and, although susceptible to frost in harsh conditions, is worth a place in the garden if you can find it a sheltered spot. The reverse of the bright cerise petals is slightly greyish-pink which adds to its unique charm and is well set off by dark red woody stems. Although it only flowers once in early summer, the blooming period is prolonged. Given the right position it can get to around 15ft, but 10ft is more common.

GUINÉE

15ft (4.6m)

◀ 8ft (2.5m) ▶

CLASSIFICATION: Climber
ORIGIN: Mallerin (1938)
COLOUR: Deepest crimson-maroon with golden
  stamens
BLOOM SIZE: Large – 4½in (11cm)
FOLIAGE: Leathery, dark green
GOOD FOR: South- or west-facing wall

Another delicate customer, but with very dark
blooms, so dark, in fact, that they can look black
(although climate and soil factors can cause
variations). This unusual colouring looks best if set
against a light background, although it looks
wonderful against mellow brick, as a backing to a
mixed border. It is a particularly good foil for blue-
flowered companion planting. Give it food and
warmth and it will reach its projected 15ft. It might
even give you a second flush of flowers in Autumn.
The fragrance is splendid, rich and sweet.

THE TITLE IS NOT meant to be disparaging but complimentary. There isn't an ugly rose among them – a robust disposition does not preclude good looks.

But from the point of view of the beginner, or someone who does not have time to coax a rose to succeed, we wanted to provide a starting point. This doesn't mean you can ignore the basic planting and maintenance advice, but no hidden foible should trip you up. Many of our most loved roses are here, and deservedly so. They are all tolerant, reliable and not particularly susceptible to any pests or diseases although our list does include 'Zéphirine Drouhin', 'Kathleen Harrop' and 'Veilchenblau' which, like many ramblers, will get mildew if they are in very dry or airless positions.

There is also a high proportion of roses which will forgive less than perfect conditions, such as poorer soils or light shade. Furthermore, owing to their popularity, some of these varieties may well be stocked by local garden centres or even found in supermarkets. Recommendations for particularly difficult conditions are also listed at the back of the book in *Which climbing rose is best for …?* (page 62).

'Phyllis Bide' (right) was an excellent choice to frame the door of this cottage. Its colouring enhances the subtle honey tones of the stone and as there is not a lot of room, a less vigorous but continuous flowering variety is essential. We can only imagine the fragrance, but it can't be too much of a hardship to sit on that bench and enjoy it. 'Phyllis Bide' has one other great boon, which is beautifully illustrated here – it has flowers from top to bottom of the plant.

'Phyllis Bide' frames the door of this tiny cottage

FÉLICITÉ ET PERPÉTUE
('Climbing Little White Pet', 'Félicité Perpétue')

15ft (4.6m)

◀ 15ft (4.6m) ▶

FRAGRANT

NORTH-FACING

POOR SOIL

CLASSIFICATION: Rambler
ORIGIN: Jacques (1827)
COLOUR: Buds stained crimson, white flowers
BLOOM SIZE: Small – 1½in (4cm)
FOLIAGE: Dark, small and neat, semi-evergreen
GOOD FOR: Pergola, arch, tripod,
    growing through trees

You can't say anything bad about this rose, except that you could be deceived by its name as it is summer flowering. In fact, Jacques' lucky daughters had it named for them. It's vigorous, has a light, pleasant primrose scent and carries great swathes of full, pompon-type flowers. It tolerates poorer soils and light shade and so is often recommended for a north-facing wall. It is best given its head, and can look fabulous swathing a sturdy pergola or grown through a tree. However it is worth thinking about companion plants in some situations, as it just flowers once.

SANDER'S WHITE
('Sander's White Rambler')

12ft (3.7m)

◀ 12ft (3.7m) ▶

CLASSIFICATION: Rambler

ORIGIN: Unknown. Introduced by Sander (1912)

COLOUR: White with golden stamens

BLOOM SIZE: Small – 2in (5cm)

FOLIAGE: Light green, glossy, small, abundant

GOOD FOR: Tall pillar, pergola, weeping standard, growing into trees

FRAGRANT

POOR SOIL

This is a very pleasing and much loved rambler. There is something very fresh about its clear, white flowers appearing around late summer. Its vigorous growth does not need to be confined to the vertical, it can provide ground cover and be allowed to trail over a sunny bank or other shrubs as well as up a pillar or pergola. It is not really suitable for a wall. Unchecked and in the right conditions it has been known to make 20ft. For those who hate gardening gloves, this rose is practically thornless.

ICEBERG, CLIMBING

15ft (4.6m)

10ft (3m)

REPEAT FLOWERING

SLIGHTLY FRAGRANT

POOR SOIL

CLASSIFICATION: Climber
ORIGIN: Introduced by Cant (1968)
COLOUR: White
BLOOM SIZE: Medium – 3in (8cm)
FOLIAGE: Light green, shiny
GOOD FOR: Pillar, bower, trellis, pergola, arch

Almost thornless stems make it a good choice for growing over a porch, round a door, or over an arbour (as in the photograph on the contents page) especially as it has a pleasant light fragrance. Seen growing in a shady position, the flowers gleam out from the shadows, and are very striking. There is some dispute over its capacity to flower more than once in the season, but although it may not bloom profusely after the first crop in early summer, it is rarely without something until autumn, when it sometimes has a second flush. It has even been seen with a couple of blooms weighed down by snow in January! You might have to keep an eye out for mildew and blackspot.

SOMBREUIL, CLIMBING

13ft (4m)

◀ **8ft (2.5m)** ▶

CONTINUOUS

VERY FRAGRANT

CLASSIFICATION: Climber
ORIGIN: Robert (1850)
COLOUR: Creamy-white, sometimes flushed
   with pink in the centre
BLOOM SIZE: Large – 4in (10cm)
FOLIAGE: Lush, dark green
GOOD FOR: Warm wall, pillar, arch, pergola

Graham Stuart Thomas writes of it 'to be treasured
for all time' and it is definitely one for those who
love their old roses. I would defy anyone to walk
past it without stopping. It has a beautiful full
flower, bursting with petals, and a wonderful
fragrance. Again, it is often called repeat flowering,
but in practice it seems to be continuous. It will
flourish on a warm wall, but it is completely hardy
so doesn't need one. In fact as it's so easy to grow,
it's a bit of a mystery why it isn't more popular.

NEW DAWN
('Everblooming Dr W van Fleet')

15ft (4.6m)

◀ 10ft (3m) ▶

CONTINUOUS

FRAGRANT

NORTH-FACING

POOR SOIL

DISEASE RESISTANT

CLASSIFICATION: Climber (Modern)

ORIGIN: Introduced by Somerset Rose Nurseries (1930)

COLOUR: Blush, with yellow stamens

BLOOM SIZE: Medium – 3in (8cm)

FOLIAGE: Glossy, mid-green

GOOD FOR: Pillar, pergola, arch, fence or wall

One of Britain's favourite roses, and it's not difficult to see why. It really is tough as old boots, easy to grow and widely available. Subtle pearly colouring, pleasing, continuous flowers, arching growth and healthy-looking foliage make it a great choice for an enormous array of structures or positions. Interestingly enough, although a sport of Dr W Van Fleet and not a cultivar this was the first rose to receive a patent. It looks particularly lovely grown with the sky-blue clematis 'Perle d'Azur'.

MADAME ALFRED CARRIÈRE

20ft (6.1m)

◀ 10ft (3m) ▶

CLASSIFICATION: Climber
ORIGIN: Schwarz (1879)
COLOUR: Creamy-white, with hint of pink
BLOOM SIZE: Medium – 3in (8cm)
FOLIAGE: Pale green, large, abundant
GOOD FOR: Scrambling through trees, trellis, pergola or wall

CONTINUOUS

FRAGRANT

NORTH-FACING

POOR SOIL

Although it is not a truly pure white, for it has a hint of pink in the buds, it is one of the best of the 'whitish' climbers. Strong and beautiful with few thorns, there are many examples of its smothering a wall in a fabulous display of scented blooms – the cottage at Sissinghurst for one. This is best at the beginning of the season, waning after mid July while it gathers energy for a second go in September. A sunny wall would be the best choice for it to really shine, but it will tolerate, and is frequently recommended for, north-facing sites as well.

MEG

12ft (3.7m)

◀ **12ft (3.7m)** ▶

REPEAT FLOWERING

VERY FRAGRANT

CLASSIFICATION: Climber (Modern)

ORIGIN: Gosset (1954)

COLOUR: Pale apricot-pink, large, dark-yellow stamens

BLOOM SIZE: Large – 5in (13cm)

FOLIAGE: Large, plentiful and dark

GOOD FOR: Pergola, pillar or wall, scrambling over bushes or hedges

This is not a good choice for those who like their flowers diminutive. The leaves and wavy-petalled flowers are large, but elegant nonetheless. The colour is very beautiful, but has more pink than apricot. This is another rose which might even be best grown over hedges or other shrubs, as long as they are sturdy enough to bear the weight. The blooms do, rather sporadically, repeat but must be encouraged by dead-heading. They have a rich and pleasing fragrance. It looks at its best early in the season.

CÉCILE BRUNNER, CLIMBING

25ft (7.6m)

◀ 20ft (6.1m) ▶

CLASSIFICATION: Climber
ORIGIN: Hosp (1894)
COLOUR: Pale, shell pink.
BLOOM SIZE: Small – 1½in (4cm)
FOLIAGE: Abundant, bright green
GOOD FOR: Growing through trees, clothing
buildings, very sturdy pergolas, big walls

A sport of Cécile Brunner, the tiny scrolled buds
open to full, urn-shaped flowers with a delicate
fragrance. Initially these are borne singly and then
later in open sprays. The first flush in mid-summer
is the most impressive, lasting several weeks, but
becoming a little unreliable thereafter. It is often
recommended for difficult situations, such as poor
soil or light shade. It's very vigorous and can achieve
great heights. Its luxuriant foliage is disease free.
A winner.

SLIGHTLY FRAGRANT

POOR SOIL

DISEASE RESISTANT

ALOHA

8ft (2.5m)

◀ 6ft (1.8m) ▶

CONTAINER

CONTINUOUS

VERY FRAGRANT

DISEASE RESISTANT

CLASSIFICATION: Climber (Modern)
ORIGIN: Boerner (1949)
COLOUR: Rose-pink with coppery tones.
BLOOM SIZE: Medium – 3½ in (9cm)
FOLIAGE: Plentiful, leathery, dark green
GOOD FOR: Pillar, low wall, small gardens,
    cut flowers

This is the perfect choice for the small space.
You can even grow it in a large container, but do
not attempt to use it to fill a large area as you will
have to wait a long time for it is quite a slow
grower. It has a pleasing strong, spicy fragrance,
disease-resistant, bronzy foliage and two flushes
of bloom in a season, with plenty of flowers in
between. The young flowers have more than a hint
of orange, and the petals have a darker reverse. As
it is so short, it can be grown as an arching shrub
to great effect. Prune only lightly.

COMPASSION
('Belle de Londres')

10ft (3m)

◀ 8ft (2.5m) ▶

CLASSIFICATION: Climber (Modern)
ORIGIN: Harkness (1973)
COLOUR: Salmon-pink tinted with
   apricot-orange
BLOOM SIZE: Large – 4in (10cm)
FOLIAGE: Plentiful, large, glossy, dark green
GOOD FOR: White wall, fence or pillar
   in smaller gardens

CONTAINER

REPEAT FLOWERING

VERY FRAGRANT

NORTH-FACING

DISEASE RESISTANT

For the admirer of the Hybrid Tea, this is one of
the best climbers available, with perfectly formed,
shapely flowers. These cloak the rose from the
bottom up and come in two flushes, both generous,
at the beginning and end of the season, and often
with something in between. However, it is probably
its fragrance which inspires the most devotion.
Combine these qualities with ease of growth,
plentiful and healthy foliage and it is easy to see
why it has become so very popular, and comes so
highly recommended.

PHYLLIS BIDE

8ft (2.5m)

◀ 5ft (1.5m) ▶

CONTAINER

CONTINUOUS

FRAGRANT

NORTH-FACING

POOR SOIL

CLASSIFICATION: Rambler
ORIGIN: Bide (1923)
COLOUR: Pale creamy-yellow flushed with pink
BLOOM SIZE: Small – 2in (5cm)
FOLIAGE: Shiny, light green, pointed leaflets
GOOD FOR: Wall, arch, pillar

There are always exceptions to every rule, and if you're excited by such things, this is a rambler which reliably flowers throughout the season. What this means is that you get the benefits of lovely lax, branching rambler-type growth that looks so well on arches and pergolas, without the drawbacks of a fantastic flush followed by nothing. It is an ideal pillar rose, as it is not too tall, and the clusters of charming flowers are not confined to the top of the plant, but clothe it to the base.

GLOIRE DE DIJON
('Old Glory')

15ft (4.6m)

◀ 12ft (3.7m) ▶

CLASSIFICATION: Climber
ORIGIN: Jacotot (1853)
COLOUR: Buff, pink tints later
BLOOM SIZE: Large – 4in (10cm)
FOLIAGE: Semi glossy, mid green
GOOD FOR: Warm wall, arch, pergola

REPEAT FLOWERING

VERY FRAGRANT

NORTH-FACING

To see it at its best, a warm sunny wall is the place,
but like many of the roses in this section, it will
also tolerate a north wall. The leaves have a reddish,
burnished quality when young, branching growth
holding generous, quartered flowers of an unusual
and elegant buff colour. Nearly a century and a half
old, it is still widely available, and much loved,
bringing pleasure not only through its form, but
also its fragrance. Warm weather can turn the
flowers slightly pinkish, which isn't really a flaw.
A great rose and widely available.

CONSTANCE SPRY

12ft (3.7m)

◀ 10ft (3m) ▶

VERY FRAGRANT

POOR SOIL

CLASSIFICATION: Large-flowered Shrub Rose
    (English Rose)
ORIGIN: David Austin (1961)
COLOUR: Rich pink
SIZE: Large – 5in (12cm)
FOLIAGE: Dark green
GOOD FOR: Generally grown as a shrub,
    but better as a climber

It's a fair cop. 'Constance Spry' is not strictly
speaking a climbing rose, but as it is able to achieve
12ft or more, and looks wonderful when treated as a
climber, it seems churlish to leave it out. It
illustrates how arbitrary is the line drawn between
some shrubs and climbers. It has splendidly
generous, cupped blooms stuffed with petals,
reminiscent of a peony, a strong spicy scent and is a
forebear of many of David Austin's acclaimed
'English Roses'. It's definitely worth having a peek
at it if visiting Mottisfont Abbey (see *Gardens to visit*
page 59), where it looks staggering.

VEILCHENBLAU
('Violet Blue')

12ft (3.7m)

◀ 7ft (2.2m) ▶

CLASSIFICATION: Rambler

ORIGIN: Schmidt (1909)

COLOUR: Purple violet, white at centre with
yellow stamens

BLOOM SIZE: Small – 1 inch (2.5cm)

FOLIAGE: Glossy, light green

GOOD FOR: Wall, arch, pillar, scrambling
through smaller trees, north-facing walls

FRAGRANT

NORTH-FACING

POOR SOIL

Forgive the tendency to mildew. You can easily
reduce the risk by planting it in light shade, the
colours are better and it is nice to find a rose that
actually does better in it. The real enticement is
that the blooms of 'Veilchenblau' make an attractive
progression from purple to dark violet and then lilac
grey. An unusual and special colouring for a climbing
rose. It has a fresh and fruity fragrance. A good
example of this is at Kiftsgate (see *Gardens to visit*
page 59).

ZÉPHIRINE DROUHIN
('Thornless Rose')

9ft (2.8m)

◀ 6ft (1.8m) ▶

CONTAINER

CONTINUOUS

VERY FRAGRANT

NORTH-FACING

POOR SOIL

CLASSIFICATION: Climber
ORIGIN: Bizot (1868)
COLOUR: Cerise-carmine
BLOOM SIZE: Medium – 3in (8cm)
FOLIAGE: Mid-green with a sheen
GOOD FOR: North-facing wall, trellis or
     pillar in sunnier sites

This is an incredibly popular rose, and can even be
found in some supermarkets. However it is also
susceptible to mildew, a condition much helped by
growing it against a north-facing wall. This deficit
is more than matched by the fabulous quantity and
continuity of its blooms, if dead-headed regularly,
and a blissful, sweet, rich fragrance. This latter
characteristic means it will never pass unnoticed in
the garden. It has very attractive reddish shoots and
as the alternative name suggests, it is almost
thornless – a nice bonus if grown over a porch or
around a door. It makes a striking pairing with the
dark purple *Clematis viticella*.

KATHLEEN HARROP

8ft (2.5m)

◀ 6ft (1.8m) ▶

CLASSIFICATION: Climber
ORIGIN: Discovered by Dickson (1919)
COLOUR: Shell pink
BLOOM SIZE: Medium – 3in (8cm)
FOLIAGE: Mid-green, semi-glossy
GOOD FOR: North facing wall, trellis or
   pillar in sunnier sites

CONTAINER

CONTINUOUS

VERY FRAGRANT

NORTH-FACING

POOR SOIL

It is interesting that after a visit to Mottisfont,
where it was blooming furiously when almost
everything else was over, it became a favourite
of one of the compilers of this book. It goes to
show that no guide will ever compete with the
experience of seeing a rose growing in situ.
'Kathleen Harrop' is a sport of 'Zéphirine Drouhin'
(opposite) and is like it in most respects, although
it has a softer, more subtle colouring and darker
leaves. It shares the tolerance for a north wall, the
unbelievable fragrance and thornless characteristics
of its parent.

CRIMSON SHOWER

12ft (3.7m)

◀ 7ft (2.2m) ▶

CONTINUOUS

SLIGHTLY FRAGRANT

CLASSIFICATION: Rambler
ORIGIN: Norman (1951)
COLOUR: Deep crimson
BLOOM SIZE: Small – 1¼in (3cm)
FOLIAGE: Plentiful, small, shiny,
    bright green leaflets
GOOD FOR: Pillar or weeping standard

Large swathes of crimson flowers with a light but
sweet fragrance bloom from midsummer and
continue into September. Its rich, unfading colour
is complemented by the backdrop of glossy leaves. It
can be grown on a fence, but its flexible stems and
generous flowering habit make it ideal for a pillar or
weeping standard. It is interesting to note that
Norman was a British *amateur* rose breeder.

ÉTOILE DE HOLLANDE, CLIMBING

15ft (4.6m)

◀ 15ft (4.6m) ▶

CLASSIFICATION: Climber
ORIGIN: Leenders (1931)
COLOUR: Deep crimson
BLOOM SIZE: Large – 5in (13cm)
FOLIAGE: Abundant, deep green, matt
GOOD FOR: Large, sunny wall or fence

REPEAT FLOWERING

VERY FRAGRANT

This is one of the most reliable of the crimson
climbers, a sport of the bush Hybrid Tea, and the
velvety flowers are so profuse and smell so heavenly,
arguments about whether it is a continuous or
summer flowering rose don't matter that much. You
will probably get most of the flowers in the summer,
but some (lucky) people have had it go on and on. It
does need sun and fertile moist, well-drained soil to
thrive, so give it some space on a south or south-
west facing wall.

Companion plants

It is particularly useful to plant something that will enhance,
or take over from, a climbing rose, particularly when it is clothing
a structure such as a pergola or arch, or other focal point you don't
want to look barren and sad when the rose is not in flower. Some
overlap with the flowering period of the companion plant is a good
idea, or you can just plant something that will flower alongside it.
A yellow rose with little scent, for example, would work well with
summer jasmine that has extremely fragrant white flowers from June
to September. Another stunning combination is a deep pink rose,
like 'Zéphirine Drouhin' grown next to a purple-leaved vine, the
foliage of which changes throughout the season from claret-red to
deep purple. Pillar roses look wonderful with lavender or nepeta
(catmint) at the base and sweet peas can be grown up bare rose
stems. But perhaps the most perfect combination is with clematis.

If you want to complement both flower size and colour,
some of the smaller-flowered *viticella* varieties look very lovely –
'Abundance' (pinky-red), 'Royal Velour' (dark purple), 'Étoile
Violette' for example, but other suggestions are C. 'Jackmanii
Superba' with red or yellow roses; 'Perle d'Azur' (sky blue);
'Comtesse de Bouchaud' (pink); 'Elsa Späth' (deep blue – May to
September); 'Ernest Markham' or 'Niobe' (deep red – July to
October); 'Lady Northcliffe' (wedgwood blue – works well in a
container); *C. orientalis* (yellow bells and wonderful seed heads – July
to October); 'Marie Boisselot' (white – May to October).

Another approach to companion planting involves using plants
with properties which will benefit the roses in other ways. For
example, sweet peas will enrich the soil. Catnip will keep it moist in
summer but dies back, allowing mulching to take place in Autumn.
Pungent herbs, such as lavender or thyme may help keep away pests.
Chives and garlic seem to help against black spot and also deter
aphids. Cranesbill geraniums encourage hoverfly which are even
better at aphid-eating than ladybirds. This approach to companion
planting will not give you overnight results, but is very rewarding.
Bob Flowerdew's *Complete Book of Companion Gardening* (details in
bibliography) is a very enjoyable read on this subject. The HDRA
(see page 61) also provides leaflets for a nominal fee.

Gardens to visit

Take a notebook and a pen. Many of these gardens label both the roses and the companion plants – and you'll probably get lots of ideas.

David Austin Roses
Bowling Green Lane
Albrighton
Wolverhampton WV7 3HB
Tel: (01902) 376300

Peter Beales Roses
London Road
Attleborough
Norfolk NR17 1AY
Tel: (01953) 454707

Castle Howard
Nr York
North Yorks YO60 7DA
Tel: (01653) 648444

Gardens of the Rose
(The Royal National Rose Society)
Bone Hill
Chiswell Green
St Albans
Hertfordshire AL2 3NR
Tel: (01727) 850461

Hidcote Manor (National Trust)
Hidcote Bartrim
Nr Chipping Camden
Gloucestershire GL55 6LR
Tel: (01386) 438333

Kiftsgate Court
Chipping Camden
Gloucestershire
Tel: (01386) 438777

Mannington Hall
Nr Saxthorpe
Holt
Norfolk
Tel (01263) 584175

Mottisfont Abbey (National Trust)
Nr Romsey
Hampshire SO51 0LP
Tel: (01794) 340757

Nymans Garden (National Trust)
Handcross
Nr Haywards Heath
West Sussex RH17 6EB
Tel: (01444) 400321

Queen Mary's Rose Gardens
Regent's Park
London NW1
Tel: (020) 7486 7905

Rosemoor Garden Charitable Trust
Great Torrington
Devon EX38 8PH
Tel: (01805) 624067

Sissinghurst Castle (National Trust)
Nr Cranbrook
Kent TN17 2AB
Tel: (01580) 712850

Wisley Garden
(Royal Horticultural Society)
Woking
Surrey GU23 6QB
Tel: (01483) 224234

A number of private gardens open every summer under The National Gardens Scheme. A guide is published which can be obtained from bookshops, or local papers often feature gardens open in the area. Cuttings can often be bought (as well as excellent teas). The proceeds go to charity.

Rose nurseries

Most will provide catalogues on request.

Acton Beauchamp Roses
Acton Beauchamp
Worcester WR6 5AE
Tel: (01531) 640433

Apuldram Roses
Apuldram Lane
Dell Quay
Chichester
West Sussex PO20 7EF
Tel: (01243) 785769

David Austin Roses
Bowling Green Lane
Albrighton
Wolverhampton WV7 3HB
Tel: (01902) 376300
Orders: (01902) 376377

Peter Beales Roses
London Road
Attleborough
Norfolk NR17 1AY
Tel: (01953) 454707

Cranborne Manor Garden Centre
Cranborne
Wimborne
Dorset BH21 5PP
Tel: (01725) 517248

Cants of Colchester Ltd
Nayland Road
Mile End
Colchester CO4 5EB
Tel: (01206) 844008

James Cocker & Sons
Whitemyres
Lang Stracht
Aberdeen AB15 6XH
Tel. (01224) 313261

Dickson Nurseries Ltd
Milecross Road
Newtownards
Co. Down
Northern Ireland BT23 4SS
Tel (01247) 812206

Fryer's Nurseries Ltd
Manchester Road
Knutsford
Cheshire WA16 0SX
Tel: (01565) 755455

Gandy's Roses Ltd
North Kilworth
Nr Lutterworth
Leicestershire LE17 6HZ
Tel: (01858) 880398

R Harkness & Co Ltd
Cambridge Road
Hitchin
Herts SG4 0JT
Tel: (01462) 420402

C & K Jones
Goldenfields Nursery
Barrow Lane
Tarvin
Cheshire CH3 8JF
Tel: (01829) 740663

E B LeGrice (Roses) Ltd
Groveland
Thorpe Market Road
Roughton, Nr Cromer
Norfolk NR11 8TB
Tel: (01263) 833111

Mattocks Roses
The Rose Nurseries
Nuneham Courtney
Oxford OX44 9PY
Tel: (0345) 585652

Notcutts Garden Centres Ltd
Head Office
Tel: (01394) 44544
(Ring to find nearest location)

Scotts Nurseries (Merriott) Ltd
Merriott
Somerset TA16 5PL
Tel: (01460) 72306

St Bridget Nurseries Ltd
Old Rydon Lane
Exeter
Devon EX2 7JY
Tel: (01392) 873672

J A Steele & Sons
(inc. Lagan Valley Nurseries) Ltd
The Market Place
Regent Street
Newtownards
Co. Down
Northern Ireland BT23 5AD
Tel: (01247) 818378

Henry Street Nursery
Swallowfield Road
Arborfield
Nr Reading
Berks RG2 9JY
Tel: (01189) 761223

Stydd Nursery
Stoneygate Lane
Ribchester
Nr Preston
Lancashire PR3 3YN
Tel: (01254) 878797

This is just a selection. A more comprehensive list is available in a publication called Find That Rose, compiled by the British Rose Growers Association which is updated annually. For more information send a SAE to Angela Pawsey, 303 Mile End Road, Colchester, Essex CO4 5EA.

Other useful addresses

The Royal Horticultural Society
80 Vincent Square
London SW1P 2PE
Tel: (020) 7834 4333
Website: www.rhs.org.uk

Membership includes free access to gardens, information about, and special rates for RHS shows, and discounted rates for horticultural courses, lectures and workshops taking place all over the UK.

Royal National Rose Society
(address as on page 59)
Tel: (01727) 850461

Membership includes a free quarterly journal, handbooks on rose varieties, free entry to the Gardens of the Rose and other gardens and reduced price entry to shows

The Henry Doubleday Research Association (HDRA)
Ryton Organic Gardens
Coventry CV8 3LG
Tel: (01203) 303517

Probably the best source of inspiration for those who wish to garden organically. A membership information pack is available from the above number, but includes a free quarterly newsletter, free entry to gardens (including RHS gardens) and access to courses, help and advice.

Which climbing rose is best for ...?

This list is a selection of roses described in this book.

	Poor Soils	North Walls	Growing into trees and disguising ugly structures
Alexander Girault	■		■
Cécile Brunner, Climbing	■		■
Compassion		■	
Constance Spry	■		
Dublin Bay	■		
Félicité et Perpétue	■	■	■
Gloire de Dijon		■	
Golden Showers	■	■	
Iceberg, Climbing	■		
Kathleen Harrop	■	■	
Madame Alfred Carrière	■	■	
Maigold	■	■	
Mermaid		■	
New Dawn	■	■	
Phyllis Bide	■	■	
Sander's White	■		■
Veilchenblau	■	■	■
Zéphirine Drouhin	■	■	

Bibliography

Allison, Sally *Climbing & Rambling Roses*
(Moa Beckett 1993)

Austin, David *The Heritage of the Rose*
(The Antique Collectors' Club Ltd 1988) – now available updated in two
volumes *Old Roses and English Roses* and
Shrub Roses and Climbing Roses

Beales, Peter *Classic Roses*
(Collins Harvill 1985)

Beales, Peter *Twentieth Century Roses*
(Collins Harvill 1988)

Flowerdew, Bob *Complete Book of Companion Gardening*
(Kyle Cathie 1993)

Fretwell, Barry *Clematis as Companion Plants*
(Cassell 1994)

Gibson, Michael *Fifty Favourite Roses*
(Cassell 1995)

Gibson, Michael *Growing Roses*
(Croom Helm Ltd 1984)

Harkness, Jack *Roses*
(J M Dent & Sons 1978)

King, Peter (editor) *The Good Gardens Guide*
(Ebury Press – revised annually)

RHS *A-Z Encylopedia of Garden Plants*
(Dorling Kindersley 1996)

RHS Plant Guide: *Roses*
(Dorling Kindersley 1996)

Scarman, John *Gardening with Old Roses*
(HarperCollins 1996)

Stuart Thomas, Graham *The Graham Stuart Thomas Rose Book*
(John Murray 1994) – incorporating *The Old Shrub Roses*, *Shrub Roses of
Today* and *Climbing Roses Old and New*

Warner, Chris *Climbing Roses*
(Century Hutchinson 1987)

Photography credits and copyright

Index

VERY OFTEN, the site in which you wish to plant your rose is the deciding factor in which rose to buy. Nurseries are always being asked to advise on this. Using the most commonly-asked questions as a starting point, all the roses in this book have been graded by the characteristics which seem to matter most to us. These icons and buttons have been arranged down the side of each rose entry to act as a quick reference when making a short-list of possible contenders for a place in your garden.

The icons

POSITION

Needs a sunny position

Will tolerate only half a day's sun, but give it the most you can

CLIMATE

Half-hardy
Can withstand temperatures down to 0°C (32°F)

Frost hardy
Can withstand temperatures down to -5°C (23°F)

Fully hardy
Can withstand temperatures down to -15°C (5°F)

SIZE

Height of plant from ground

Spread of plant